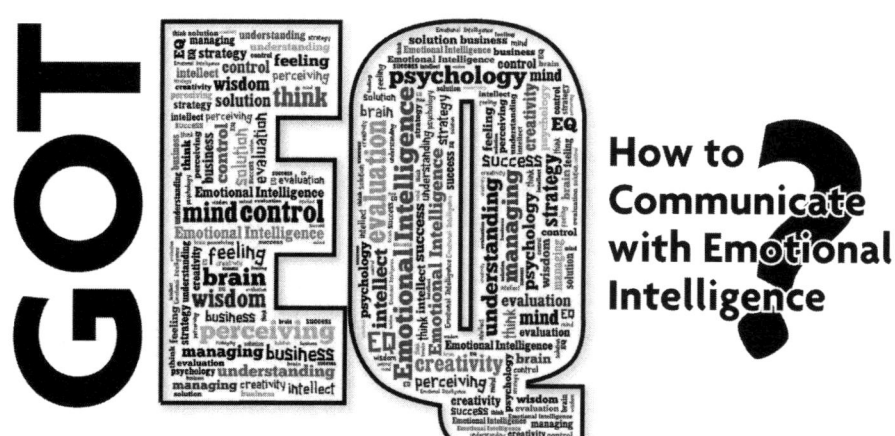

How to Communicate with Emotional Intelligence

Pamela Jett

GOT EQ?

How to Communicate with Emotional Intelligence

Copyright © 2015 by Pamela M. Jett

Published by

Perfect Bound
Marketing + Press

www.PerfectBoundMarketing.com

Graphic Designer | Brandi Hollister

ISBN 978-1-939614-60-5

Printed in the U.S.A.

Become the

MASTER

of your emotions.

Do not let

YOUR EMOTIONS

be the master of you.

This book is for *you* if...

- You want to be more promotable.

- Success in your current position is important to you.

- You want to be the master of your emotions and not have your emotions be the master of you.

- You want to improve your relationships—both at work and at home.

- Creating a better quality of life matters.

The ability to communicate with **emotional intelligence** can make or break success in every area of life. Emotionally intelligent people are more promotable, have better working and personal relationships, and are, overall, better equipped to deal with challenges and obstacles.

And yet many people are not sure what **emotional intelligence** is, or how to **get it**, **improve it**, and **use it**. If you want to harness and improve the power of your emotional intelligence—your **EQ**—this book is the resource you need.

Loaded with tools, tips, and techniques you can use immediately, this book will give you a better understanding of what EQ is, show how to enhance yours and, most importantly, help you use your EQ to enhance your communication.

So, What *is* Emotional Intelligence?

Emotional intelligence has many different working definitions. Here is a particularly useful one:

Emotional intelligence is the ability to
identify, understand, manage, and use emotions
in positive and constructive ways.

Let's break that definition down into its various parts.

- Identify emotions

- Understand emotions

- Manage emotions

- Use emotions

Emotionally intelligent people have competencies in each of these areas.

IDENTIFY EMOTIONS

Emotionally intelligent people are self-aware enough to recognize emotions as they are experiencing them. Additionally, they are able to differentiate between emotions, such as understanding the difference between feeling angry and feeling frustrated, even though those emotions can often be very similar.

UNDERSTAND EMOTIONS

In addition to being able to identify emotions, emotionally intelligent people understand those emotions. They know the key drivers of those emotions. For example, they not only can accurately determine whether they are angry or frustrated, they know why they are frustrated (or angry.)

MANAGE EMOTIONS

Emotional self-awareness makes it easier for emotionally intelligent people to manage emotions. For example, someone may feel angry. However, that person is still able to behave in a reasonable and rational way. A person can feel the emotion and then choose how to communicate and behave.

USE EMOTIONS

Emotionally intelligent people are able to channel emotional energy into communicating and behaving in a way that can enhance relationships and drive positive results. They don't try to eliminate their emotions. Rather, they use emotions in positive and constructive ways.

How to Use this Book

The research is *very clear:* Emotional intelligence can be learned and improved. No matter your current level or EQ, you can always take it to greater levels of effectiveness.

There is a therapeutic school of thought known as cognitive behavioral therapy (CBT.) The basic (very simplified) premise of CBT is that if you act "as if," the feelings will follow. For example, if you want to "feel" more connected to your partner, act the way connected partners act by holding hands, etc. This is a perspective to use in developing your EQ.

Perhaps your level of EQ isn't as high as you would like it to be. Take on some of the tools presented in this book. Decide to "act" like an emotionally intelligent person, even if it is profoundly different from your current patterns and habits. Over time, those actions and internal choices will become your "new normal" and viola! You are more emotionally intelligent!

This book has very distinct sections that correspond to each component of emotional intelligence. You can read it straight through. Or, you can skip to the area that you would like to focus on. Another option is to read the tips and techniques at random.

It's important to note that some of the tools, tips, and techniques can be seen as relevant in boosting skills in more than one area of EQ. So something placed in one section might also be applicable in another section.

Because these tools provide great fodder for discussion, you will find assistance in creating discussion around each tip in appendix A at the end of this book.

IDENTIFY
Emotions

Build Your Emotional Vocabulary

Perhaps no tool will improve your EQ faster than building your emotional vocabulary. Many adults have very limited emotional vocabularies. Or we only use a very limited portion of the emotional vocabulary we possess.

Why does this matter? It's simple. If we only have one word, such as anger, handy to label the myriad of emotions we can experience, we are likely to grab that word. The result? A lot of emotional subtly is lost.

For example, if you are feeling annoyed, but you label what you are feeling as anger you make it more difficult to manage that emotion (another component of EQ.)

Emotionally intelligent people strive to label the emotions they experience as accurately as possible. This requires a more diverse and varied vocabulary than the typical "go to" words (or labels) of *anger, happiness, sadness, etc.*

One way to improve the accuracy of labeling your emotions is to build your emotional vocabulary. Actively seek out and use new (or at least different for you) words to describe what you are experiencing.

For example, the next time you experience an emotion you are tempted to label "anger" or you think to yourself: *I am so angry,* check yourself and ask yourself if perhaps one of the following is a more accurate description:

- Frustrated

- Annoyed

- Confused

- Overwhelmed
- Irritated

Obviously, these are only a few of the options.

Emotionally intelligent people have a varied emotional vocabulary—build yours!

Label Your Emotions Accurately

Clearly, having a well-developed emotional vocabulary helps with this process. Emotionally intelligent people understand the power of labels.

If you label what you are feeling internally as "sadness" then everything you experience at that time will be filtered through the lens of "sadness." Imagine how your experiences might change if you realized you aren't really feeling "sadness" and that perhaps it is boredom or melancholy?

Accurate labels can lead to better choices to alleviate or manage those negative emotions. Check in with yourself and strive to label your emotions accurately.

Create a "Feelings List"

Create a "master feelings list." Perhaps keep this "feelings list" in your journal or someplace else where you can easily access it. That way, if you are having a feeling that you are struggling to identify, it serves as a handy cheat sheet.

Sometimes It's Simple...

And sometimes it's not. Emotionally intelligent people know that it is possible to feel more than one emotion at the same time. They acknowledge that complexity rather than try to deny it.

Embrace Duality

Not only is it possible to experience more than one emotion at the same time, it is also possible for those emotions to seemingly contradict each other.

For example, you might simultaneously be happy for a colleague who got a promotion while also feeling sad (or even jealous) that it wasn't given to you.

Rather than try to discount or invalidate one emotion in favor of another, emotionally intelligent people are able to embrace the duality and honor both emotions as being valid and reasonable.

The Power of *And*

It's helpful when you are attempting to recognize multiple emotions to use the word *and* instead of the word *but* in your self-talk.

> *"I'm really happy Chris was promoted and I am jealous."*

That way you won't be discounting or minimizing one emotion in favor of another.

Nix the Judgment

Sometimes it is tempting to judge, blame, or shame ourselves when we identify an emotion that we may not be proud of such as *jealousy, anger, fear, etc.*

Emotionally intelligent people know that experiencing a negative emotion doesn't make them bad people. When they identify an emotion they try to simply accept it as their reality at that given moment.

It is vitally important to recognize that experiencing an emotion is profoundly different from acting on that emotion. There will be more about that later.

Failing to identify emotions, even the negative ones, can lead to even greater challenges later. Repressed emotions can lead to physical ailments, more difficulty managing behavior later on, and psychological challenges.

Your thoughts...

UNDERSTAND
Emotions

Two Primary Emotions

Emotionally intelligent people know that there are two primary negative emotions: anger and fear. All other negative emotions are in a subset of these emotions. And while it is important when naming emotions to be exact and move beyond the two primary emotions, knowing whether you are feeling anger or fear (or both) can help you understand what is driving or causing those emotions.

Take a moment and ask yourself: *Am I feeling fear, anger or both?* It's a quick way to understand what is going on internally.

Ditch a Few Assumptions

Build your emotional intelligence by learning to differentiate between how you "feel" about a situation and the objective situation itself. In others words, remember that your feelings are not always accurate gauges of what is going on.

For example, in a conversation with a friend you may "feel" criticized and hurt. However, that may not be what your friend intended.

That doesn't mean you don't have a right to feel criticized and hurt. It means that emotionally intelligent people are able to know there might be another way to interpret the situation.

Question your assumptions and boost your EQ!

Honor Your Internal Locus of Control

Emotionally intelligent people understand that their feelings are not caused by external factors such as other people, events, or circumstances. Rather, they know that they are the ultimate determiners of how they feel. They honor their internal locus of control.

This means that they don't expect other people to make them happy. They know happiness is an internal choice.

They understand that no one can make them feel guilty unless they agree to it.

Emotionally intelligent communicators don't play the victim with *"you make me mad"* and other similar blaming statements.

This is not necessarily easy because some situations (or people) seem to have a lot of power and influence over how we feel. Emotionally intelligent people recognize that even in extreme cases, they still get to choose how they feel.

Feel The Fear and Do it Anyway

In addition to understanding that fear is a primary emotion, emotionally intelligent people don't assume that feeling fear means they are making a mistake or a poor choice.

Rather, they understand that fear is a signal to pay attention, to learn, to notice, and to decide. Fear is a natural response to change or to things that are new or challenging. Feeling fearful doesn't necessarily mean you will fail or ought not to continue.

Emotionally intelligent people don't let fear paralyze them. They feel fear. They acknowledge the fear. Learn from the fear and decide to either adjust course or feel the fear and do it anyway!

Know Your Body

Emotions tend to show up in physical ways:

- Tense muscles
- Tummy trouble
- Increased heart rate
- Shortness of breath
- Headache
- Sweat
- Many others

Emotionally intelligent people pay attention to these signals.

Not only does this increase self-awareness, it can serve as a powerful clue as to what triggers emotions in the first place.

For example, I sometimes feel a physical sensation of being so tense that I feel squeezed. When I feel that way physically, it's a powerful signal to me that I am feeling overwhelmed.

Awareness of that physical sensation then better equips me to make choices to alleviate commitments or to change my schedule.

What is your body trying to tell you?

H.A.L.T.

Emotionally intelligent people understand their "triggers," or what events tend to trigger particular emotional responses. One quick way to check in with yourself when you start to feel intense emotion is H.A.L.T.

H.A.L.T. works on two levels. The first is that to say (or think) "halt" gives you a moment of space between stimulus and response. We will discuss more about the importance of creating this space in a later tip.

The second level is that H.A.L.T. is an acronym that can allow you to better understand your emotions.

Stop and say to yourself *"H.A.L.T."* and do a quick check-in with yourself.

H – HUNGRY

Check and ask yourself: *Am I hungry?* When we are hungry we tend to become more easily triggered emotionally.

This has led to the pop-culture term *hangry*. Sometimes you aren't really angry (or whatever other intense emotion you are experiencing.) You are simply hungry. Take care of that physiological need and your emotions will often settle down.

A – ANGRY

Sometimes, your emotional response to an event is genuinely driven by the core of anger and it is good to be aware.

L – LONELY

Lonely is related to the primary emotion of fear. Fear of not being included, of not being part of things, fear of missing out—all can sometimes trigger loneliness. This knowledge can also help you address the root causes of your emotions.

T – TIRED

If you are like most people, when you are tired *everything* can seem more intense. Check in with yourself and ask: *Am I tired?* If the answer is yes, then you can take the necessary steps, like a nap, to prevent a meltdown.

We've all seen children freak out when they are tired. Sometimes, adults do the same.

H.A.L.T. is a great tool to help you understand your emotions and what might be triggering them. Try it the next time you feel your emotions are getting the better of you.

Keep a Journal

Interested in better understanding your emotions? Keep a journal. Record what you feel, the intensity of those feelings, and the events that led up to those feelings.

Be observant. Look for patterns. For example, if you regularly get annoyed or frustrated at work, journaling might help you discover that meetings that are poorly run are a trigger or conversations that revolve around budget issues are a source of frustration.

While this understanding doesn't change the triggering events, it can help you better prepare for those events.

Understand the Power of Your R.A.S.

Your reticular activating system, a.k.a. your R.A.S., plays a powerful role in communicating with emotional intelligence. Your R.A.S. serves as a filter. We are inundated all day long with data, stimuli, and information. So much so that we can't possibly process it all.

Your R.A.S. serves as a filter, determining what information will register with you and what will not. A common example of your R.A.S. in action is when you buy (or even just do internet research about) a new vehicle. All of a sudden, you start seeing that exact same vehicle everywhere! It's not that there are suddenly more of those vehicles on the road, it's that they are now registering with you as they never have before.

Your R.A.S. plays a key role in your EQ. If you expect to be irritated by someone or something, your R.A.S. will actively seek out data to prove you right. It's at the core of self-fulfilling prophecies.

Emotionally intelligent people recognize the role their perceptions (guided by their R.A.S.) have on emotions *and* they use that understanding to question the accuracy of their perceptions and their corresponding emotional responses.

Your thoughts...

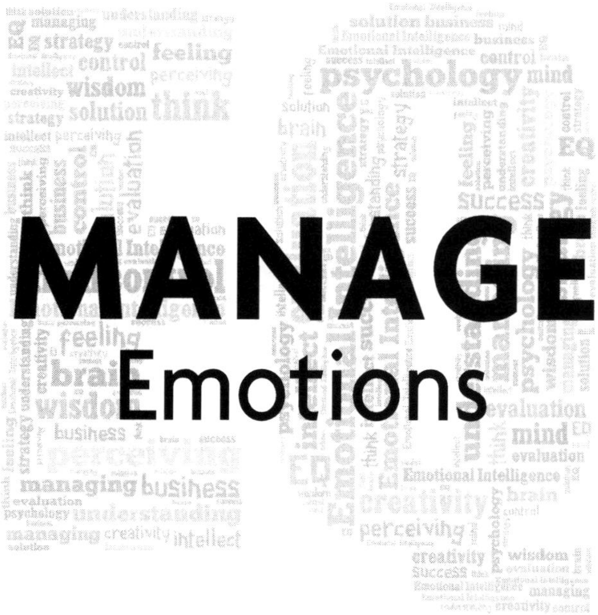
MANAGE
Emotions

Happiness... It's Optional

While emotionally intelligent people understand they are responsible for their own happiness and understand the power of choosing to be happy, they don't need to choose to be happy *all the time*.

They honor a wide variety of emotions, even the negative ones. They don't demand that they constantly maintain a state of joy. Rather, they can live in the ebb and flow of a full range of emotions.

And, they can choose to be happy when that is the option that serves them best.

Management vs. Suppression

It's easy to confuse emotional intelligence with completely unflappable composure. Emotionally intelligent people are not *always* calm, cool, and collected. They don't manage their emotions to the point that they completely suppress them.

Rather, emotionally intelligent professionals choose the when, where, and how of emotional expression. They may decide to have an emotionally charged conversation at the time and place of their choosing instead of flying off the handle or expressing everything that pops into their heads in the moment.

Next time you are about ready to engage in an intense conversation, ask yourself: *Is this the when, where, and how I want to have this conversation?*

Choose Friends Wisely

We all need confidants, people to whom we can express our (true) feelings. We all need people with whom we feel free (and safe) to share the broad spectrum of our emotions, not just the ones that are desirable or that fit with our "image."

Emotionally intelligent people chose those confidants wisely. They know that trust and intimacy take time to develop. While they are friendly with many, they are mindful of who they allow into their minds and hearts.

I learned this lesson the hard way. Many, many years ago (I was in graduate school) I trusted someone way too early with something very personal regarding my feelings as an adopted child. My expectation was that I would receive support, validation, and perhaps some empathy. That is *not* what happened. Instead of support, her response felt like a punch to my solar plexus. It literally knocked the physical (and emotional) wind right out of me.

At that moment I realized: *Oops! She is not the right person to trust with sensitive information.* Lesson learned.

Choose your friends, your source of social support, wisely.

A Bad Day Doesn't Equal a Bad Life

Have you ever met someone who thinks that because he is going through a rough patch (or even simply having a difficult day) that it means he is doomed? This slippery-slope type of thinking is avoided by emotionally intelligent people.

People with strong EQ know that: *This, too, shall pass*, and that: *Tomorrow is another day*. They allow themselves to be fully present in the "bad day," but they don't assume it means they have a "bad life" or are headed for disaster.

Reaction vs. Response

One of the most crucial skills emotionally intelligent professionals possess is the ability to respond to situations rather than react to them.

When we react to external stimuli, or have an external locus of control, we give up our power to choose. Reaction implies that you have no choice or power.

In stark contrast, when we respond to external stimuli we are operating from an internal locus of control. Emotionally intelligent people understand that to respond means to choose. And that is empowering.

It means that regardless of how others are behaving or what events are happening we have the ability to decide how it is going to impact us and how we will behave.

For example, emotionally intelligent people don't yell simply because someone else is a yeller. Rather, they choose whether yelling or a different response is more likely to give the results they are looking for in the conversation.

Embrace the Space and Choose Choice!

Viktor Frankl, Holocaust survivor, psychotherapist, and author of Man's Search for Meaning (a must-read, from my perspective) taught that *"Between stimulus and response there is a space. In that space lies our freedom and power to choose our response. In our response lies our growth and freedom."*

People with high EQ embrace this space and they make a choice to choose their responses.

They ONLY way this is possible is to have different response options to choose from. If all you know to do when someone yells is to yell back, it's not possible to choose a different response. This leads to our next tip for building EQ...

Get a Wrinkly Brain

Did you know, every time you learn something new you get a new wrinkle in your brain? These have a scientific name. They are called neuro-pathways. I like to think of them as brain wrinkles. In fact, I am so enamored of the "brain wrinkles" concept that I send out a regular "Brain Wrinkles" newsletter loaded with tools, tips, and techniques. To sign up, visit http://jettct.com/brain-wrinkle-signup/.

Emotionally intelligent people know that in order to respond as opposed to react, they need response options or skills. They are committed to learning new skills on a regular basis.

Build your EQ by building your skills. Invest in your own education and professional development.

Want to respond more effectively or have more response options to deal with a yeller? Go to a workshop on dealing with difficult people. Register for a webinar, read a book, read a blog, listen to a podcast or an audio program. There are webinars available to you at JettWebinars.com and communication resources available at my Success Store located at http://jettct.com/success-store/. Check them out and build your response options.

Stop waiting for your leader to send you to seminars or to register you for a conference. Of course, when they do, go!!!! Commit to taking the lead in your own skill development.

Set aside time and resources for learning and you will be building your EQ in the process.

Manage Your Self-Talk

In that space between stimulus and response you can help yourself make wise choices by managing your self-talk in the moment. We all talk to ourselves. Emotionally intelligent communicators take charge of the voice in their head and manage their self-talk.

There are several keys to making self-talk work for you. The following tips can help you make the most of the voices in your head.

Delete

This first tip for managing self-talk is to recognize negative self-talk when it's happening and do something proactive to change it.

One way to do this is to say to yourself: *Delete,* or: *Cancel,* or: *Erase* when you find yourself in a negative spiral. Don't allow the negative voice to reign.

Call Yourself Names

Your name, that is. The latest research reveals that if you call yourself by name, almost as if someone else is talking to you, your self-talk will have greater impact.

For example, when I am doing intentional self-talk I often say something like: *Pamela, you've got this,* or: *Pamela, you are calm.*

Plant the Positive

Self-talk is very powerful and emotionally intelligent people choose what they say to themselves wisely. They speak in terms of desired behaviors as opposed to undesired behaviors. They speak in terms of positive behaviors, not negatives.

For example, emotionally intelligent would say:

- *"Jane, you're calm"* instead of *"you're not upset."*

- *"Pat, you're patient"* instead of *"you're not impatient."*

- *"Jeff, you're competent"* instead of *"you're not an idiot."*

Present Tense

Emotionally intelligent communicators who want to engage in better responses will leverage their self-talk and make sure self-talk is in the "present tense" not the future.

For example, people with high EQ say these sorts of things to themselves:

- *"Ellie, you are patient"* instead of *"you will be patient."*

- *"Sam, you are kind"* instead of *"you will be kind."*

Using the present tense coupled with name calling and desired behavior give people with high EQ the edge in believing the things they say when they talk to themselves.

Proactive Frame Questioning

Framing is a very simple psychological concept that says as human beings we tend to organize (frame up) events that happen in our lives and create some sort of explanation or story for those events. For example, if your significant other brings you flowers you could "frame" that experience in different ways. One way might be to think: *He loves me and wants me to feel special.* Another way might be" *I wonder what she did wrong now?* Both interpretations of the event could be right. And, both could be wrong. We base our frames upon previous experiences or "frames of reference."

Emotionally intelligent people know that there can be more than one way to "frame up" an event and they proactively question their frame by asking themselves questions such as:

- *Is there an alternate story?*
- *What else could be going on here?*
- *Is there another way to look at this?*

These are not the only frame-changing questions you can use. You can also ask yourself frame-changing questions specific to a current situation. For example, if you are thinking something is a crisis you can challenge that by asking: *Is this a crisis?* Or, if something seems to be a very big deal, try: *Will this matter in 15 years? (or even 15 minutes?)*

Challenging your current way of looking at a situation can help you see it in a different light. This doesn't mean your original frame is wrong. In fact, there is no one right way to frame any situation. It's more a question of if your current frame serves you. If not, try proactive questions to change your frame.

Be Relentless

Be relentlessly positive, that is. Emotionally intelligent people tend to be positive in action and in disposition.

Not to be confused with being a "Pollyanna" or not being willing to face things that are difficult or negative, communicators with high EQ start from a positive place unless the evidence shows them otherwise.

This is the foundation of "realistic optimism" which people with high EQ practice. It makes it so much easier to manage emotions if they are, in general, positive.

Again, this isn't to be confused with being delusional or ignoring problems. Rather, it is about looking at a problem or challenging situation and trying to see it in the most positive light possible.

For example, change can be difficult. However, people with high EQ will see the challenges of the change along with the growth opportunities.

Be relentlessly positive. And, the good news? Research indicates that this gets easier with practice!

Q-TIP!

QTIP stands for Quit Taking It Personally. People with strong EQ avoid a phenomenon known as "negative personalization." In other words, they don't take everything personally.

For example, imagine a friend or colleague hasn't returned your call or text. Instead of assuming something negative such as: *They must be mad at me*, or: Clearly, they are too busy for a peon like me, try looking for alternative, less personal, explanations such as: *They must be caught up in a big project*, or: *Perhaps my message got lost in the shuffle.*

People with high EQ can remind themselves to do this by saying "QTIP" to themselves any time they engage in negative personalization.

Your thoughts...

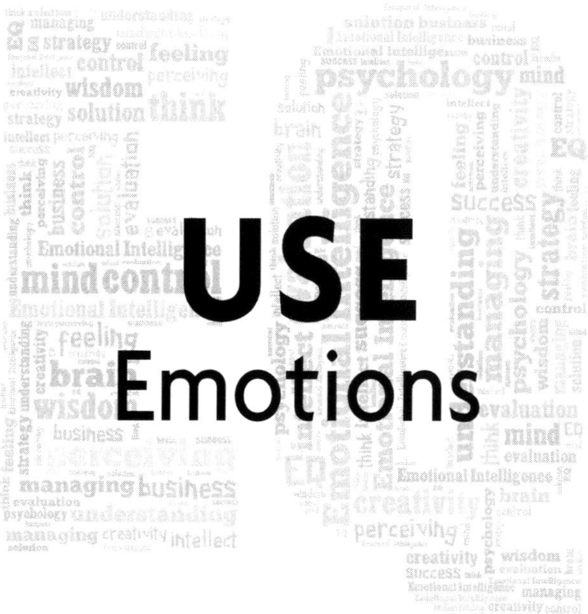

USE
Emotions

Practice Internal Gratitude

Research is very clear: Emotionally intelligent people actively look for things to be grateful for in any given situation or as a way to adjust their mood on the fly.

The next time you feel your mood start to slip, ask yourself: *What am I grateful for?* The amazing news is that neuro-scientific research makes it clear that finding your gratitude isn't what is most important. What's most important is remembering to look in the first place. The act of looking for things to be grateful for makes neurons in the "happiness" part of your brain more efficient. Bottom line: Being grateful makes your brain happy!

There is also substantial evidence that gratitude, specifically gratitude towards others, increases activity in the social dopamine circuits of the brain. This makes social interactions more enjoyable!

Practice External Gratitude

In addition to remembering to be grateful internally, people with high EQ express gratitude.

Tell people you appreciate them and what they do. Be conscientious about saying thank you. Write thank you notes.

One of the benefits of this practice is that it often creates what is called a "positive feedback loop." You express gratitude to others and it helps them feel better or more positive. This increases the likelihood they will say and do positive things to you.

Forgive

Emotionally intelligent people know that holding on to anger, resentment, and bitterness is a poor choice. Holding a grudge or holding on to anger, and even continuing to feed that anger, can be destructive physically, emotionally, and relationally.

The relational damage isn't limited to the person at whom you are angry. You can develop a reputation as the kind of person who holds grudges or is very slow to forgive. That can negatively impact other relationships.

Forgiveness isn't to be confused with being a doormat or someone who lacks boundaries. Rather, forgiveness is about no longer allowing hurt, anger, and frustration to direct your choices. It is possible to forgive someone and resume a positive relationship. And it is also just as possible to forgive someone while simultaneously learning from the (likely negative) experience and make different choices regarding how much you will trust or interact with that person in the future.

Emotionally intelligent people know that failing to forgive ultimately hurts them more than anyone else.

Stop Waiting on the Apology

No doubt about it: It is far easier to forgive someone who offers an apology. It takes tremendous strength to forgive someone who has yet to, and perhaps never will, admit to doing something hurtful or inappropriate.

The concept of QTIP (quit taking it personally) was introduced in a previous section of this book. Our ability to QTIP is drawn from overcoming something known as "fundamental attribution error." Essentially, it is human nature to blame someone's behavior on a personality trait ("they are so rude") or to make it about ourselves ("they must not like me") instead of blaming a situation ("they must be headed to a tough meeting" or "perhaps they had a rough morning"). Fundamental attribution error means we make things personal instead of situational.

Because we are all susceptible to fundamental attribution error, we will sometimes view a failure to apologize as "pure selfishness" or "total insensitivity" or "they are so mean."

Emotionally intelligent people are aware of fundamental attribution error. They catch themselves and try to reframe the situation with something like: *Maybe they really don't realize it was hurtful*, or: *Maybe they are going through a lot right now.*

Obviously, reframing in this way doesn't make the actions of others less painful. However, it can make it easier to forgive, even when someone doesn't apologize.

Forgiveness is powerful. It allows relationships to grow and develop and it keeps the negative from taking control.

Who are you waiting to forgive? What are you waiting for? If it's an apology, considering forgiving anyway.

Practice Reflective Listening

Emotionally intelligent people understand that the message heard isn't always the message that was sent (or intended). Miscommunication is a key driver of problems and conflicts at work and at home.

Emotionally intelligent people don't assume that what they heard is accurate. They use reflective listening to reduce miscommunication. In a world where many things are simple, but not easy, reflective listening is both simple *and* easy.

Reflective listening is when you relay your understanding of what someone just said with phrasing such as:

If I understand you correctly, you want...

I want to make sure I got it. What you are essentially saying is...

The reflective listener completes statements like these with a paraphrasing of what they just heard.

Crucial point! Sometimes the reflective listener will paraphrase something and the speaker will correct them with:

That's not what I said.

Or, *That's not what I meant*

Or, even the brutal, *No, you're wrong. I didn't say that.*

Emotionally intelligent communicators will not take the bait and get defensive. Rather, they will respond with something like:

Ok, help me to understand. Tell me more.

One of the key elements in this approach that emotionally intelligent communicators are keenly aware of and use intentionally is keeping the responsibility of understanding on their own shoulders and not blaming the speaker for being unclear. They avoid saying things like:

You're confusing me.

You need to be more clear.

And, emotionally intelligent people avoid getting into an argument with responses such as:

Um... That IS what you said!

Yes, you did.

Emotionally intelligent communicators are more concerned with understanding than with being right. And, they are willing to use reflective listening to create shared meaning.

Practice Verbal Empathy

In contrast to sympathy, which means to feel sorry *for*, empathy is the ability to feel *with* someone. It is the ability to put yourself in someone else's position and feel what they are feeling.

Earlier segments of this book contain tools such as reframing that can help you build empathy. Emotionally intelligent communicators verbalize that empathy.

They use statements such as:

Wow, that must be hard.

Oh, that would make me nervous too.

If I were in your shoes I would feel the same way.

And while tempting, emotionally intelligent communicators try to avoid the trite:

I understand.

Especially saying "I understand" all on its own. While saying "I understand" is a form of empathy, people typically need more in order to really feel understood.

And, as the late great Stephen R. Covey taught, the deepest need of the human soul is to be understood. Practice more verbal empathy and your relationships will be the better for it.

Assume Positive Intent

Emotionally intelligent people know that communication and interactions run more smoothly when we start from an assumption of positive intent.

Assume that people you are dealing with mean well, even if the way they communicate might be awkward or even slightly difficult. Start with the mindset that they are coming from a place of trying to be helpful, not hurtful. Let positivity be your starting mindset.

Obviously, not everyone you interact with has positive intent. However, emotionally intelligent people start with positive. This baseline assumption can be particularly helpful when reading email.

We all know that people sound more harsh and intense in email. Someone with low EQ might be quick to assume that someone is angry and fire back an angry response. Assuming positive intent allows you to not take offense so quickly.

Assuming positive intent can also be very helpful when our conversational partner is very emotional and perhaps isn't choosing words wisely and carefully. We are less likely to let their words trigger an emotional escalation in us.

Assuming positive intent can also help us work around our personal "hot spots." For example,

I really don't like it when people say to me "you shouldn't feel that way" when I'm talking about something that is painful or upsetting. That phrase sends a message of "you don't have a right to your own feelings." I don't feel validated, respected, or understood. I admit it. I am hypersensitive to this phrase.

I also know that in the vast majority of situations, the speaker has NO IDEA of having been very hurtful and disrespectful. The intention was to be helpful, not hurtful.

By remembering to assume positive intent I am less likely to get irritated at somene for not being the kind of empathetic listener I need at that moment. Instead, I'm able to take what is offered in the way it was intended.

In what situations would assuming positive intent help you?

Perhaps when you are working on a project with someone from another team who has a very direct communication style that seems abrasive to you?

Perhaps when peers deliver some "criticism," advice, or feedback on a project that is inaccurate because they don't know the whole story or have all the facts?

Perhaps when you want to respond defensively to an email?

Assuming positive intent doesn't mean you will keep that assumption in place. However, when you start there, interactions are typically more positive and productive.

Decide

Emotionally intelligent people are deciders. They don't wait to feel 100% sure or for things to be perfect. They know that the act of deciding and taking forward motion is powerful. Brain science shows that making decisions, even imperfect decisions, reduces worry and anxiety as well as increasing problem solving.

Making decisions can be (okay, *is*) hard. Recognize that it's okay to make "good enough" decisions. Emotionally intelligent communicators know that trying to be perfect overwhelms the brain with emotions and can make a person feel out of control.

Decide. Communicate your decision. And, recognize that you can always tweak or adjust or even completely reverse your decision if necessary.

After all, it was your decision in the first place. You can always decide something else.

By freeing yourself up to change your mind, you often free yourself up to move forward.

And, brain science teaches us that we don't just choose things we like, we end up liking the things we choose.

What does that mean? It means the act of deciding can help you see more of the benefits, payoffs, and positive ways of leveraging your decision.

What decision are you putting off making? What are you waiting to be perfect before you take action? Decide to decide and move forward!

Have a Plan B (and C and D)

Emotionally intelligent communicators know that having contingency plans makes it so much easier to decide and take action.

Think ahead and have options in case things don't go exactly as planned. Having a back-up plan will help you feel more confident and less stressed.

When communicating plans to your leader, talk about your contingency plans. Not only will this build confidence in your decision, it will also boost your credibility in decision making. Even if she doesn't like your plan, your leader will be more likely to encourage you to tweak or adjust that plan because she has more confidence in your abilities.

If you are leader, communicate your initial plan and consider communicating your contingency plans to your team. This will help them feel more confident in you and your leadership. And if you really want to boost their confidence, give your team the opportunity to contribute to (or even create) the plans.

Fail Forward

Emotionally intelligent people not only understand the importance of "failing forward," they are able to talk or communicate about their failures in a "forward" way.

They take each failure and frame it as a learning experience. That doesn't mean they ignore negative repercussions from errors, mistakes, or failures. However, emotionally intelligent people strive to learn from each mistake and apply that knowledge to future endeavors.

If that is your mindset, then use future-focused communication when discussing the failure. For example, if your leader calls you out for a mistake you can respond by saying something like:

Yes, I made a mistake. Here is what I learned...
and this is what I will do differently next time...

Notice, there is no excuse making, defensiveness, or blaming (a sign of low emotional intelligence). Rather, there is acceptance and then a transition to the future.

You can even use this technique when you communicate with yourself (your self-talk). If you make a mistake at work, instead of beating yourself up on the drive home, spend some time thinking about what lessons you learned and what you will do differently in the future.

Your leader is looking for team members who are able to acknowledge and learn from mistakes. Use future-focused communication and "fail forward."

Accountable Communication

Emotionally intelligent communicators avoid the blame game and use accountable communication, especially when communicating about their own feelings and emotional state. That means they avoid using phrases such as:

You make me so mad!

You make me so frustrated!

They are so annoying!

You make no sense.

The common denominator in each of these examples is a shifting of responsibility. Emotionally intelligent people, while willing to express emotions, don't do it in a way that gives away their power and puts the blame on someone else.

Rather they use accountable communication and make statements such as:

I am angry.

I am frustrated.

I get annoyed when...

I'm not understanding what you are saying.

The common denominator in this form of communication is the "I am" statement. This doesn't mean you would never let someone know the part they play by saying something like:

I get angry when you...

It hurts my feelings when you...

When... I feel frustrated.

The key element is taking ownership of your emotional response to their behavior. This is an assertive communication technique. There are myriad assertive communication techniques that emotionally intelligent people use. To add more to your communication repertoire, see appendix B.

Choose Battles Wisely

One of the key ways emotionally intelligent professionals differ from those who are not is they understand which issues they can control or influence and which are outside their control or influence. They choose to expend their energy and efforts toward things they can actually do something about.

This doesn't mean that they don't ever become upset about things out of their control, such as weather ruining a planned outing. However, they recognize that there is a limit to how much emotional energy such a disruption merits.

And they try to keep their communication focused on things they can do something about, as opposed to things they can't. So instead of whining about how upset they are about the rain, they might mention they are upset and then move on to planning something else to do instead.

This may seem like a small thing. However, if you've ever dealt with someone who goes on and on about things they can do nothing about you know how significant it is.

Keep the focus of your communication on those things you can impact and you will be viewed and treated like (and actually be) a professional who can move projects forward, who is decisive, who is a problem-solver, and who is an overall positive professional.

Your thoughts...

Your thoughts...

FINAL
Thoughts

Emotionally intelligent people know that becoming the master of their emotions and not letting their emotions be the master of them is the foundation for great communication.

Emotionally intelligent communicators are able to leverage their self-awareness into better relationships, higher levels of productivity, and more success at work. International search firm Egon Zehnder International analyzed 515 senior executives and discovered that those strongest in emotional intelligence were more likely to succeed than those strongest in either IQ or previous experience.

The good news is that EQ is a skill set that can be improved. Use the tools and techniques in this book, build your EQ, and begin to reap the rewards at work and at home!

Appendix A

To get the most out of this book, why not use it to stimulate discussion with your team? Ensure sure each team member has a copy of the book. For bulk order discounts call 866-726-5388.

Choose a tip or tips you would like to discuss as a way, perhaps, to open a team meeting. Give people a chance to read and ponder the tip or tips under discussion. When you convene your team, here are a few discussion questions you can use. Pick one or two, or use them all.

- How will this tip help you as you work with customers? Peers? Your team?

- What other areas aside from work could this tip impact?

- What might make using this tip or technique difficult?

- What, if any, drawbacks could using this tip create?

- What steps will you take to remind yourself of this technique?

- In what situations will you practice this tip?

- Who could you share this tip with? How would you share it? How might it benefit them?

Appendix B

The following assertiveness resources may help you build your assertive communication ability.

- Subscribe to Pamela's "Brain Wrinkle" for regular assertiveness updates at http://www.jettct.com/brain-wrinkle-signup/

- Read Pamela's blog at http://www.jettct.com/blog/

- Check out audio and video resources at http://www.jettct.com/success-store/communication-success-series/

- Visit JettWebinars.com for instant online training or to register for live webinars.

Appendix C

Download our complimentary EQ assessment and discover your personal EQ strengths and opportunities for growth at JettCT.com/EQ

Book Pamela Jett to Speak at Your Next Meeting or Event!

Bring the powerful and engaging communication tools in this book to your group or team! Pamela conducts fast-paced, interactive, and skill-building sessions for groups of any size. Depending on your objectives and constraints, Pamela can tailor her message of remarkable communication to fit your time frame and your group's core needs. Pamela's presentations zero in on the "words to use" and the "words to lose" so that professionals can reap the rewards of higher productivity, better teamwork, less turnover, and enhanced bottom-line results.

For more information, call 866.726.5388.

For a complete list of programs available, visit JettCT.com

Want More? How About a Webinar?

Experience Pamela's powerful tools for professional success during one of her popular webinars. Webinars are:

- Cost-effective

- Great for groups

- Easy to access

Every webinar comes with a download so you can learn at a time and place that works best for you!

Visit JettCT.com today to view the current schedule of webinars and to register.

For information on customized webinars call 866.726.5388.

About Pamela Jett

For more than two decades, Pamela has been helping professionals become better leaders, communicators, and team players. With an emphasis on building communication skills, leveraging positive attitude, and enhancing employee engagement, Pamela's live presentations, books, and audio programs are loaded powerful tools for everyday success!

Additional Resources by Pamela Jett
Available at JettCT.com/success-store

*Communicate To Keep 'Em: enhancing employee
engagement through remarkable communication*

This book packs a big punch when it comes to developing remarkable communication skills that will enhance employee engagement. With a focus on practical application, language patterns, and specific "words to choose" and "words to lose," you will discover communication tools you can put to use immediately.

*What to Say? 7 Secrets of Remarkable Communication
for Remarkable Results*

It's no secret—communication is your most important skill.

In this powerful audio CD program, discover seven secrets of remarkable communication for remarkable results so you can more confidently know what to say—even during your most difficult conversations.

Mind Your Own Business: A Career Management System

It's a myth that "good work gets noticed." To receive the attention, authority, and the respect you deserve, you must manage your own career success. In this fast-paced and entertaining audio CD program, you will develop a strategy to "mind your own business" and succeed.

Communicate With Confidence, Credibility and Influence

As a professional woman you want others to see you as strong, competent, and capable. Discover effective communication tips on how to master confident communication to achieve the results you desire.

Success is An Attitude

All great success starts with one fundamental—the right attitude! Everyone in your organization can benefit from this DVD program and discover how to efficiently manage their attitude for great success, productivity, and teamwork.

**Looking to share what you've learned?
Call 866.726.5388 and ask about bulk order discounts.**

Connect with Pamela Jett

 Pamela Jett

Pamela Jett, CSP

Pamela Jett

 PamelaMJett

Pamela Jett
Jett Communication Training, Inc.
P.O. Box 7385
Mesa, AZ 85216

866.726.5388

JettCT.com

contact@jettct.com

Your thoughts...

Your thoughts...